IS THAT A FACT?

Did Castles Have Bathrooms?

And Other Questions about the Middle Ages

ANN KERNS

ILLUSTRATIONS BY **COLIN W. THOMPSON**

LERNER PUBLICATIONS COMPANY

Minneapolis

Contents

Perhaps you've heard beliefs like these about the Middle Ages:

Medieval kings made people knights by tapping them with swords!
Kids in medieval times married at age twelve!

But are these beliefs true? Is there anything to the stories you've heard? Come along with us as we explore the Middle Ages. Find out whether our perceptions of the time are **FACT OR FICTION!**

Are the Middle Ages the Same as the Dark Ages?

NOPE. But they did overlap some. In Europe, the Middle Ages lasted in most countries from about A.D. 500 until the late 1400s. The Dark Ages spanned the years 500 to 1000.

The terms *Middle Ages* and *Dark Ages* were made up by historians in the late 1400s. They lived at the beginning of an era called the Renaissance. Renaissance people admired ancient Greece and ancient Rome. They didn't care too much about the time between the ancient world and their own day. So they lumped all those centuries together and called them the Middle Ages. The Middle Ages are also called the medieval period.

YAWN

Renaissance historians thought no one cared about learning or art during early medieval times. So they called that period the Dark Ages (by "dark," they meant unenlightened). But modern historians think the trash talk about the early Middle Ages isn't true. So many stopped using the phrase *Dark Ages*. Instead, they divided the Middle Ages into three periods: the Early Middle Ages (500–1100), High Middle Ages (1100–1300s), and Late Middle Ages (late 1300s–1400s in most countries). Lots of our ideas about knights and castles come from the High Middle Ages.

Did Medieval Knights Really Joust?

YES! You've probably seen knights jousting (fighting on horseback) in cartoons or in the movies. And they jousted in real life too. Jousting was part of a contest called a tournament. Jousts and tournaments were popular forms of entertainment in the Middle Ages. Everyone from kings to peasants came to watch.

Did You Know?

People still joust. Mock battles are often staged at outdoor events called Renaissance fairs (left). Some modern jousters wear armor to re-create medieval tournaments. Others wear modern clothes and use their lances to grab three small rings while galloping down the field.

Tournaments began as a form of training. They kept knights in shape for war. At first, the most popular part of a tournament was the melee. In a melee, teams of knights and foot soldiers fought in open fields. Melees could get pretty wild. They were a little *too* much like real battles. Many contestants were hurt or even killed. So tournaments became more organized— and somewhat safer. They were fought before an audience on a smaller field.

In the High Middle Ages, jousts became popular. In a joust, two knights rode their horses at each other. They were separated by a low fence called a tilt. The goal was to knock your opponent off his horse with a lance (a long spear). Jousts were held for entertainment. That's why the lances were made of breakable wood, and their tips were blunted. Still, getting knocked off a galloping horse with a big stick was no picnic.

So why did knights do it? Tournaments and jousts were good ways to make money. Being a knight was expensive. A knight had to have costly armor, weapons, horses, and a whole crew of people to help him. A tournament winner could take home money, armor, and horses. He could become a famous soldier. And he might even draw the attention of a rich noblewoman in search of a dashing husband.

7

Did People in Medieval England Talk As We Do?

NOPE. Pretend you've hopped into a time machine and traveled back to medieval England. Could you just walk up to people and start chatting away? Not a chance! You'd have a hard time understanding them. And they'd have a hard time understanding you.

Languages change over time. The English we know is Modern English. In England during the High Middle Ages, people spoke Middle English. Middle English was influenced by three other languages—German, Latin, and French.

Middle English grew out of Old English, also called Anglo-Saxon. The Angles and the Saxons were people from modern-day Scandinavia and Germany. They spoke versions of the Germanic language. In the A.D. 400s, these groups began invading the British Isles. As they settled in Britain, their languages mixed to become Anglo-Saxon.

Latin was the language of the Roman Catholic Church. Church services were held in Latin. Schools were taught in Latin, and most books were written in that language.

So how did French get into the mix? In 1066 Britain was invaded by a French nobleman, William of Normandy (*right*). William declared himself the king of England. And he became known as William the Conqueror. He spread Norman French culture and language throughout England.

As if the German-Latin-French mix wasn't enough, some people also spoke local versions of Middle English. So you'd have to study your medieval phrase book pretty hard before you got in that time machine.

Say What?

Can you understand these words from Middle English? Some you may be able to guess. For others, have a look at the Modern English translation.

MIDDLE ENGLISH	MODERN ENGLISH
bord	dinner table
fauntekyn	small child
gulden	golden
jape	joke, trick
kechyn	kitchen
poke	bag, sack
scole	school
sey sooth	tell the truth
wood	crazy

Did King Arthur Really Rule England during the Middle Ages?

NO. In fact, historians aren't even sure whether King Arthur was a real person! But if he was real, he would have lived in the sixth century. In the stories about Arthur, he was a great hero. He defended Britain against invading armies sweeping down from mainland Europe.

From about A.D. 70 until the 500s, Britain was ruled by the Roman Empire. Then groups from northern Europe, such as the Saxons, began to take over Roman territories. People in the British Isles struggled to keep out these invaders.

The legendary Arthur was born at a time when all seemed lost for Britain. By the 600s, Saxons, Angles, and others had settled in Britain. Anglo-Saxon kings ruled the land. But in Arthurian tales, Arthur defeats the Saxons and becomes the high king.

In the 500s and 600s, Britain had no castles and no knights in shining armor. But stories about King Arthur are filled with castles and knights. Why is that? Well, many Arthurian tales actually come from the twelfth century. By then, castles and knights were common in Britain. Medieval storytellers added these details to Arthur's legends.

The storytellers also added magic and mystery. In many tales, Arthur was raised by a magician named Merlin. Arthur carried the magical sword Excalibur. He married the beautiful Guinevere, and they lived in a castle called Camelot.

A large round table stood in Camelot's great hall. Arthur invited the best warriors in the kingdom to sit at the table with him. These Knights of the Round Table became the king's loyal followers. Tales about Camelot, Guinevere, and the knights became an important part of Arthurian legend.

King Arthur sits with the Knights of the Round Table in this fifteenth-century illustration.

Did Most People Die Very Young during the Middle Ages?

Many young men in medieval times died from war injuries.

YEP, THERE'S A LOT OF TRUTH TO THIS ONE. People in the Middle Ages lived, on average, until the age of thirty. Disease, injury, and starvation were common causes of death.

A medieval apothecary (a person who makes and sells drugs for medical use) brews a remedy in this illustration.

Several times during the Middle Ages, Europeans experienced severe, long-lasting food shortages called famines. People relied on food grown and raised locally. If bad weather ruined the crops in the field, it could spell disaster for a community. Families soon used up their stored grain and their farm animals. Then they starved to death. Famines affected everyone—both the rich and the poor.

Disease affected everyone too. Medieval people didn't understand germs and how diseases spread. They didn't know the importance of clean water supplies, food safety, and waste disposal. As a result, outbreaks of serious diseases killed many people. Without modern medicine, even a cold could turn into a deadly lung infection. Disease took its worst toll on the very young. One in five children died before the age of five.

Young men most often died after being injured in wars or fighting. Some bled to death on the battlefield. Some died when their wounds became infected. Young women commonly died in childbirth. They, too, bled to death or developed infections. Medieval doctors used many natural medicines to treat illnesses. But they could do little to heal someone with a severe wound or a serious infection.

However, if a person survived childhood and young adulthood, he or she could live into old age. History is filled with stories of men and women still active in their forties, fifties, and beyond. In 1217 noblewoman Nicola de la Haye was put in charge of the military defense of Lincoln, England. William Marshal, a famous knight, helped her. At the time, Lady Nicola was sixty-seven, and William Marshal was seventy-one.

Is It True That Most People Couldn't Read or Write in the Middle Ages?

Begin READING

YES! For most of the Middle Ages, few people could read or write. But don't be too hard on them. There wasn't much *to* read. Books were very rare and expensive then.

The printing press was developed in Germany in the 1430s. Before that, books were all handwritten by Roman Catholic monks. Monks were religious men who lived in communities called monasteries. They copied the Bible and other sacred writings in Latin. Other religious people, such as priests, needed to at least be able to read some of the Bible. So learning to read and write became part of a person's religious training. The church ran schools where young boys learned Latin and some math and science before becoming monks and priests.

Sons of noble families who were training to be knights learned how to read and write. But their sisters usually did not. Many learned only as much reading and math as they needed to run a household.

In medieval times, Roman Catholic monks copied religious books by hand.

Most other medieval people worked on farms. They either had no need to read and write or no chance to learn. That began to change later in the Middle Ages. As towns grew, people started their own businesses. Traders and shopkeepers wanted to be able to read documents and do math. They wanted their children to learn too. Then they could run the family business. Townspeople began organizing their own schools. Education and literacy became part of the developing medieval world.

This illustration shows young boys at a monastery school in medieval times.

Did You Know?

Young medieval students spent most of the day studying Latin grammar. For that reason, learning centers for children became known as grammar schools.

Did a Terrible Plague Really Kill Millions during the Middle Ages?

YES. It was called the bubonic plague. And from 1348 to 1352, it swept through Europe and western Asia. It killed twenty-five million people. In Europe, it changed medieval society forever.

The first signs of bubonic plague were swellings in the neck and armpits. Fever, vomiting, and intense pain followed. Sores broke out on the skin and often turned black or dark blue. That earned the disease the name the Black Death. Some victims recovered, but most people died in days.

People in the Middle Ages had no idea what was causing the outbreak. But they did think that when sick people coughed, they spread the disease. This caused a panic. Many people fled their cities. Or they locked themselves in their homes. Terrified, they refused to go near the sick to help them.

By the time the Black Death ended, one-third of Europe's population was dead. This caused a severe shortage of workers on great land estates. Not enough people were left to care for the crops and livestock.

Peasants realized that the labor shortage gave them power. They could demand higher wages, more freedom, and legal rights. Rich landowners resisted the peasants' demands. But over time, the peasants won higher wages and more rights. Medieval society changed permanently.

Caused by Rats?

A common tale says that the Black Death started with the bite of a rat. Rats were common on ships. They were thought to carry diseases from faraway countries. Once the ships docked in Europe, the rats scurried into towns looking for food. They got into houses, shops, and storerooms. They bit and—so the story goes—infected people.

But rats weren't to blame for the plague. Modern doctors know that the fleas that lived on rats were the real problem. Fleas suck blood from humans and animals. When a flea infected with the plague bites, it injects bacteria into its victim's blood. And once a medieval house was infested with fleas, the fleas could travel on anything—such as pets, blankets, or clothing. That's how the Black Death spread so quickly.

Did Robin Hood Really Steal from the Rich and Give to the Poor?

PROBABLY NOT—BECAUSE HE MOST LIKELY WASN'T REAL!
But he is a very popular figure in English folklore.

This illustration shows Robin Hood and his friend Little John in Sherwood Forest.

Many Robin Hood tales date from the thirteenth century. But they are set during the time of King Richard I, from 1189 to 1199. In the Robin Hood stories, Robin is a yeoman, or small-time farmer. He's successful, but he's very unhappy about unjust laws that favor the rich. So Robin Hood takes up a life of crime to try to help poor people.

As the Robin Hood legend grew, singers and storytellers added more details. Robin fell in love with Maid Marian, a young woman from a rich family. He gained a group of followers—his band of merry men. They lived in Sherwood Forest in Nottinghamshire, in north central England.

From their forest hideout, Robin Hood and his band robbed travelers. Most of their targets were rich people who were known to be cruel or unfair. Whatever money and jewels they gained during the robberies, the merry band gave to poor peasants.

Robin and his men were outlaws. But in many tales, they were also loyal followers of King Richard. They fought against Richard's nasty brother, Prince John. And they fought against the sheriff of Nottingham, a dishonest local official.

Robin Hood remains a popular figure in books, movies, and TV shows. He's even made the jump into graphic novels. Pretty good for a twelfth-century farmer!

Did You Know?

Sherwood Forest (right) is a real place. It is more than ten thousand years old. In medieval times, the forest was 20 miles (32 kilometers) long and 8 miles (13 km) wide. It contained woodland, pastures, and small villages. The modern forest is famous for its ancient trees, its wildlife, and its importance in British history. And every summer, it is home to the Robin Hood Festival, in honor of its most famous inhabitant—real or legendary.

Is It True That Kids in the Middle Ages Married When They Were Only Twelve?

BELIEVE IT OR NOT, THEY OFTEN DID! Or at least they did in the Early Middle Ages. It was especially common for kids from rich families to tie the knot at a tender age. In other social classes, marriage ages varied a little more.

Among medieval nobility, marriage was a way to build a family's wealth and power. Noble parents arranged their children's marriages. They used marriage to build friendships between families. The families agreed to support each other in politics or war. Arranged marriages were also a way to control who inherited the family's lands.

Sometimes noble children became engaged when they were just infants or toddlers. If the girl was still a child, she often went to live with her future husband's family. The family watched over her until she was old enough to marry. If the parents were in a hurry, the girl could be married when she was as young as nine.

By the time the High Middle Ages arrived, the Roman Catholic Church had stepped in. The church began to take control of activities such as marriage. Church officials wanted to stop noble families from marrying their children off too young. The church said that both partners must be old enough to consent (agree) to the marriage. The age of consent in England, for example, was twelve years old. In England and several other European countries, noble children often married later, when they were in their midteens.

The children of middle-class and peasant families usually married when they were in their teens too. But sometimes they had to wait until they had found a good job or saved enough money. They also didn't have arranged marriages. Young women and men from peasant or middle-class homes might meet in the town market. Or they might meet after church services, at harvest festivals, and at dances. With this bit of social freedom, they were far more likely to marry for love.

People in the middle classes or from peasant families could meet their future spouses at the town market.

Did Castles Have Bathrooms?

SORT OF. But they weren't like the modern bathrooms we know, with a toilet, a bathtub, and a sink in one room. Medieval people would be amazed at quilted toilet paper, hot showers, and fluffy towels!

Instead of a toilet in a bathroom, most castles had small rooms called garderobes. The garderobe had a wooden seat with a hole cut into it. Most were built against an outside wall. Waste dropped through the hole, down a long shaft, and into a pit or into the castle's moat. To keep the smell under control, servants sprinkled the garderobes with fragrant herbs, such as lavender. People used strips of linen for toilet paper.

Peasant and middle-class homes had small outdoor toilets called privies. Peasants collected the contents of their privies and spread it in their fields as fertilizer. At least they found a good use for it!

To keep clean, people washed their faces and hands in shallow bowls. In castles, noble family members took their baths in a large wooden tub set out in the middle of a room. Often the tubs were set out in the great hall—

Medieval people took baths in wooden tubs. Servants attended to them and heated the water.

sort of a castle's version of a living room. Servants had to heat pot after pot of water to fill the tub. Rich people used soap and bath oils scented with herbs and flowers.

Bathing was very expensive, but medieval people enjoyed it. They enjoyed it so much that some larger medieval towns built public bathing houses. There, lots of people bathed together. They even played cards and games and had a few snacks while they soaked!

Medieval peasants lived a much rougher life. They didn't have servants or the luxury of hot water and scented soap. They bathed in streams. Or they washed themselves in small tubs filled with cold water.

Did Knights Begin the Custom of Shaking Hands?

NO. Some people say the practice of shaking hands goes back to medieval knights. They say that knights extended their hands to show they weren't holding any weapons. This may sound convincing, and it is a good story—but it's only a myth.

Historians think that men greeted one another with a handshake long before the Middle Ages. The ancient Egyptians, Greeks, and Romans, for example, clasped hands or forearms. This brief, friendly touch became a traditional way to show goodwill and trust. Lords and knights in medieval Europe carried on that tradition.

Kissing a person's hand is another ancient tradition that people in the Middle Ages continued. Knights and noblemen kissed the hands of royalty and high-ranking church officials. It was a sign of loyalty and respect. Medieval men also kissed the hands of noblewomen to show respect and courtesy. In return, women curtsied.

In general, medieval people valued polite, charming, and respectful behavior. Nobility and knights were very conscious of their place in society. They were eager to give and receive respect. At feasts or other gatherings, people addressed one another by title and rank, not by first names. A husband and wife might even call each other by their titles! Children always called their parents "Sir" and "Madam."

Who's Who?

Many European societies had a system of titles that reflected a person's rank. The system was complicated. But it let everyone know how to act and talk to others in society. For example, in medieval England, a king or queen was addressed as "your Highness." A duke (a high-ranking nobleman) was called "your Grace." Other noblemen and noblewomen were addressed as "my Lord" or "my Lady." Knights were called "Sir," as in "Sir Edward."

Peasants, servants, and many other workers did not have titles. They were called by their first names. For a second name, they might be called after their father, the place they lived, or their profession. For example, if Stephen made cloth for a living, he was called Stephen Weaver.

Did a Knight in Armor Weigh So Much That He Had to Be Lifted onto His Horse?

NO! Armor was clothing and gear used to protect a knight during battle. It was sturdy, but not so heavy that it kept the knight from moving freely. The image of a knight clomping around as if he's wearing a big tin can is false. So are stories that a knight's assistants had to lift him onto his horse with a crane.

Over the course of the Middle Ages, knights wore different kinds of armor. During the early period, knights usually fought with broad, heavy swords. To protect themselves from being slashed, they wore chain mail armor. Chain mail was a flexible metal fabric made of thousands of small iron rings linked together.

Chain mail was made into a hauberk (a long shirt) and a coif (a hood). A knight sometimes also wore a solid metal helmet, or helm. And underneath all the chain mail, he wore a wool garment called an aketon.

In the 1300s, knights began wearing extra protection over the chain mail. They covered their legs, hands, and chest with flat pieces of solid metal attached to fabric. These pieces were called plate armor.

But knights soon needed even more protection. Armies began using deadly crossbows. These weapons fired arrows with enough force to pierce chain mail. By 1400 knights covered themselves with complete suits of plate armor for greater safety.

The suits of armor looked heavy and stiff. But at the knees, elbows, wrists, and feet, several small plates were sewn together so the knight could move. The armor weighed about 44 to 55 pounds (20 to 25 kilograms). A knight couldn't run a mile (1.6 km) in his armor. But he could certainly get on and off his horse without any help.

Did You Know?

In battles or at tournaments, men's faces were covered by their helmets. It was hard to tell who was who. So kings, noblemen, and knights began wearing colorful tunics (long, sleeveless shirts) over their armor. The tunics displayed symbols and designs called coats of arms. The coat of arms identified the wearer. Special military officers called heralds kept track of all the coats of arms. This system of symbols became known as heraldry.

Heraldic symbols were also painted on shields and woven into flags. If a nobleman or knight was rich, even his horse wore his coat of arms! A father passed down his coat of arms to his oldest son. Other children had their own versions of the family coat of arms. Eventually, coats of arms became associated with family names.

Did Medieval Castles Have Moats and Drawbridges to Keep Enemies Out?

YES. Medieval Europe had no police to protect people. Noble families enlisted knights to live near and protect them. And the peasants lived close to the nobles and knights. They all needed a safe haven against attackers. So kings and noble families built the earliest castles as fortresses.

The earliest castles were simply wooden or stone buildings on top of a hill. At the highest point was a building called the keep. The nobleman, his family, and household servants lived in the keep. The knights, their horses, and their servants lived in buildings farther downhill. All the buildings on the hill were surrounded by an outer wall with a guarded gate.

Peasants lived in villages and on farms around the castle complex. If enemies attacked, the peasants ran up the hill to take refuge within the complex. Once everyone was safe inside, the knights locked the gates. Then they fought off the invaders from the castle's outer walls

During the Middle Ages, castles grew bigger. The keep grew from a small tower to a great house with many rooms and staircases. The outer walls rose stories high. The whole castle complex was surrounded by a moat.

This illustration of a medieval castle shows it on a hill, surrounded by a moat and high walls.

Bridges spanned the moats. The bridges could be drawn up during an attack, leaving no way for enemy soldiers to cross the moat. But if they did get across, they faced a guarded gatehouse and a heavy iron gate.

In later medieval times, attacks against castles grew less frequent. People relaxed, and homes became more about comfort than warfare. Knights and lesser nobility built their own country homes called manor houses. Manor houses didn't have moats and drawbridges. But like castles, they were centers of rural life, surrounded by villages and farms.

This castle has guard towers and is surrounded by a moat.

Is It True That Most Medieval People Never Traveled More Than a Few Miles from Home?

YES! This was especially true during the Early Middle Ages. Soldiers, nobility, and church officials traveled. But most people lived and worked on farms. Taking care of crops and animals kept them busy. They didn't have time or money for travel.

In addition, it was hard to get from place to place. There were no paved highways. Roads were rough, and travelers were at the mercy of bands of robbers. Staying home was safer than venturing out.

This lack of travel meant most people didn't know what was happening in other parts of the country. Local events, customs, and beliefs were all villagers and peasants knew.

All of this changed during the High Middle Ages. Pilgrimages became very popular. A pilgrimage is a journey to a shrine or other holy place. Some Christian pilgrims in medieval Europe traveled all the way to the Holy Land. In Christianity, the Holy Land centers on the Middle Eastern cities of Jerusalem, Nazareth, and Bethlehem. Those places are associated with the life of Jesus Christ.

Many other pilgrims traveled to sites closer to home. These sites were associated with Christian saints, or very holy people. In Britain, Canterbury was a popular destination. In Spain,

pilgrims flocked to the shrine of Santiago de Compostela. Pilgrims also often traveled to Rome, the center of the Roman Catholic Church.

To protect themselves against robbers, pilgrims traveled with a knight and his band of soldiers. Many people couldn't afford horses, so they walked. Along the way, they told stories and sang songs. They saw new sights and met other groups of pilgrims. As pilgrimages became more popular, inns sprang up to receive travelers. Pilgrimages became the guided tours of the Middle Ages!

This painting shows a pilgrimage to Santiago de Compostela in the fifteenth century.

Pilgrim Stories

In the 1380s, English author Geoffrey Chaucer began writing *The Canterbury Tales (right)*. In Chaucer's book, a group of fictional pilgrims gather in London. Together, they set off for the journey to the city of Canterbury. Along the way, the pilgrims tell stories to entertain the group. *The Canterbury Tales* was one of the first books written in everyday English. This funny, rowdy look at medieval life became a classic in English literature.

Were Medieval Peasants Slaves?

NO. Peasants were laborers who worked on landowners' estates. They tended the crops, took care of the animals, and did other jobs as needed. Landowners didn't own peasants as they would own slaves. But they often held tight control over peasants' lives.

In medieval society, land ownership meant power. Under the system called feudalism, high-ranking noblemen owned lots of land. They gave some of their land to the knights who served them. In return, each knight paid the nobleman from the profit he earned on his farm. He also promised the nobleman military support and loyalty.

The nobles and knights didn't farm their land themselves. They rented the farmland to peasants. The peasants kept some of the crops and animals they raised. But they had to give most to the landowners and to the church.

Some peasants, over time, earned enough money to buy the land they worked. But other peasants remained very poor. Among the lowest class of peasants were serfs. Serfs were bound by law to the land. A serf couldn't leave the place he was born without his lord's consent. If his lord went to war, the serf had to fight in his lord's army.

What put an end to this system? Money, for one thing. During the High Middle Ages, towns grew. Townspeople such as merchants and blacksmiths earned livings by selling goods

and services. They formed a middle class. This economic group worked and lived outside the system of lord and peasant. Land ownership was no longer the only game in town.

Peasants and serfs began moving to towns. Some found good jobs and joined the middle class. The ones left behind on the farms discovered they could demand higher pay and more rights. Well into modern times, life in the English countryside was organized around the manor house and the village. But by the end of the Middle Ages, feudalism was dying.

Working as a blacksmith or at a similar trade gave people in the Middle Ages independence.

Did Medieval Barbers Really Double as Dentists?

INCREDIBLY, YES! In the Middle Ages, barbers did more than just cut hair. They also cared for people's teeth. And they worked as doctors too. Barbers often drew blood, which was a common medieval medical treatment.

Ye Doctor/Dentist/Barber is in

Some medieval art shows dentists yanking people's teeth out with big, scary metal tools. That gave us the idea that medieval dentists were amateurs who could do only the simplest procedures. And that might have been true in many cases. But historians have found evidence that some medieval dentists did much more. They filled cavities and made false teeth. They fixed jaw injuries. And they performed surgery on patients with tongue or mouth cancer.

Unfortunately, all of these treatments had to be done without anesthetics. Those drugs that numb the pain during visits to a modern dentist didn't exist in the Middle Ages. Some herbs were used to dull pain. But even so, medieval dental work was not a fun experience.

Luckily, people in the Middle Ages didn't have soft drinks and candy bars to rot their teeth. In fact, medieval peasants probably had pretty good teeth. That's because they couldn't afford sweet food. Instead, they ate raw vegetables and whole grains.

Rich people ate more sweets. But they found ways to avoid visiting the barber (that is, the dentist). They cleaned their teeth by rubbing them with linen cloth and ashes. And they made mouthwashes of mint and pepper mixed with wine.

Wealthy people in medieval times ate more sweets than people who couldn't afford such luxuries.

Did Medieval Kings Make People Knights by Tapping Them with a Sword?

YES. That ceremony is called dubbing.

This painting from the nineteenth century shows a queen dubbing a knight.

A man was usually dubbed a knight by another knight, a lord, or by his king. The knight-to-be knelt before his lord or king. The lord tapped him on each shoulder with a sword and declared him to be a knight.

In the Early Middle Ages, soldiers who showed great courage during a battle were often made knights. A soldier could be dubbed right on the battlefield, during or after the fighting. It was an important moment for him. But there was very little ceremony.

Later, dubbing became a religious ceremony called an accolade. A knight-to-be prayed all night before his accolade. As day dawned, he dressed in his finest clothes. Then, in front of family, friends, and nobility, he was dubbed a knight. Music, dancing, a feast, and maybe even a tournament followed.

As part of becoming a knight, a man swore to obey the rules of chivalry. Chivalry was a code of behavior. A chivalrous knight promised to be loyal to the king, to honor God, and to defend the Roman Catholic Church. He vowed to treat women with respect and show kindness to the poor and the weak.

Growing Up a Knight

Many knights grew up in a sort of medieval military training program. At the age of seven or eight, a boy of noble birth went to live with another noble family. He became a page. As a page, he learned how to ride horses, shoot a bow and arrow, and fight with a sword. At about the age of twelve, the page became a squire. A squire worked for a knight, caring for weapons and horses. In return, the knight trained the squire for combat. At the age of twenty, a well-trained squire was ready to be dubbed a knight.

GLOSSARY

accolade: the ceremony by which someone officially becomes a knight

armor: clothing and gear used to protect a knight from injury during battle

chain mail: a type of protective clothing made of small metal rings linked together

chivalry: the code of behavior a medieval knight promised to obey

dubbing: the act of naming someone a knight

feudalism: a social and economic system in which land was exchanged for work or military service

garderobe: a room in a castle used as a toilet

joust: to fight on horseback as part of a staged battle

keep: the building inside a castle's fence or walls in which the owner and family lived

knight: a medieval soldier who fought on horseback

lance: a long spear

melee: a staged battle fought by knights and soldiers

moat: a ditch dug around the outside of a castle

noble: belonging to the highest social class, just below kings and queens. A man was called a nobleman, and a woman was called a noblewoman.

peasant: someone who works on a farm and owes rent and service to the landowner

pilgrimage: a journey to a shrine or other holy place

plate armor: protective clothing made of thin sheets of metal

squire: a boy in training to become a knight

tournament: a mock battle fought by knights for money or other prizes

SELECTED BIBLIOGRAPHY

Beazley, Mitchell. *The History of Europe: From the Dark Ages to the Renaissance.* London: Octopus Publishing Group, 2006.

Gies, Joseph, and Frances Gies. *Life in a Medieval Castle.* New York: Harper, 1974.

Herlihy, David. *Medieval Households.* Cambridge, MA: Harvard University Press, 1985.

Jones, Terry. *Medieval Lives.* London: BBC Books, 2004.

Time-Life Books editors. *What Life Was Like in the Age of Chivalry.* Richmond: Time-Life Books, 1997.

FURTHER READING

Burrell, Carol M. Scavella. *Did Greek Soldiers Really Hide Inside the Trojan Horse? And Other Questions about the Ancient World.* Minneapolis: Lerner Publications Company, 2011. Interested in stories about soldiers, nobility, and everyday life in ancient times? This book looks at life in ancient Egypt, Greece, and Rome.

Hanel, Rachael. *Knights.* Mankato, MN: Creative Education, 2008. Beautiful illustrations highlight this look at medieval Europe's professional fighters.

Langley, Andrew. *Medieval Life.* Rev ed. New York: DK Publishing, 2004. With plenty of color illustrations, this book covers who was who in medieval society, what people did for entertainment, and what they ate and wore.

The Middle Ages
http://www.historyforkids.org/learn/medieval
Check out this website to learn what people in the Middle Ages ate, read, believed, and did for entertainment.

Middle Ages
http://www.learner.org/interactives/middleages
This website answers the question, "What was it really like to live in the Middle Ages?" The site is divided into feudal life, religion, homes, clothing, and other categories.

Schlitz, Laura Amy. *Good Masters! Sweet Ladies! Voices from a Medieval Village.* Cambridge, MA: Candlewick Press, 2007. A pilgrim, a lord's daughter, a peasant, and twenty other young characters speak to the reader from a thirteenth-century English village. Original illustrations accompany each story.

INDEX

ACKNOWLEDGMENTS
The images in this book are used with the permission of:
© David C. Tomlinson/Photographer's Choice/Getty Images,
pp. 1, 22-23; © Jose Gil/Dreamstime.com, pp. 2 (top), 7;
© Kirill Zdorov/Dreamstime.com, pp. 2 (bottom), 17 (bottom);
© Hulton Archive/Getty Images, pp. 3 (top), 4 (bottom), 20,
23; © James Emmerson/Robert Harding World Imagery/Getty
Images, pp. 3 (bottom), 29 (bottom); © North Wind Picture
Archives, pp. 4 (top), 5, 8, 9, 15 (both), 16, 18, 25, 27, 29 (top),
35, 37; © Stock Connection/SuperStock, pp. 6-7; © Richard
T. Nowitz/CORBIS, p. 10; The Art Archive/Biblioteca Nazionale
Turin/Gianni Dagli Orti, p. 11 (both); © SuperStock/SuperStock,
pp. 12, 21, 32; © Italian School/The Bridgeman Art Library/
Getty Images, pp. 12-13; © Eric Van Den Brulle/The Image
Bank/Getty Images, p. 14; The Art Archive/Biblioteca Augusta
Perugia/Gianni Dagli Orti, p. 17 (top); © Robert Harding Picture
Library/SuperStock, p. 19; © Ivan Mikhaylov/Dreamstime.com,
pp. 24-25; © Zasranka/Dreamstime.com, pp. 26-27; © Roger
Viollet/Getty Images, p. 28; © Olivier Le Queinec/Dreamstime.
com, pp. 30-31; The Art Archive/Private Collection/Marc
Charmet, p. 31 (top); © Huntington Library/SuperStock, p. 31
(bottom); The Art Archive/British Library, p. 33; © Buyenlarge/
Hulton Archive/Getty Images, p. 34; © iStockphoto.com/Valerie
Loiseleux, p. 34 (background); © Edmund Blair Leighton/The
Bridgeman Art Library/Getty Images, p. 36.

Front cover: © Dennis Hallinan/Hulton Archive/Getty Images
(castle); © Dorling Kindersley/Getty Images (knight); © iStock-
photo.com/Tom Nulens (sign post); © iStockphoto.com/Mario
Savoia (symbols).

Lerner Publications Company
A division of Lerner Publishing Group, Inc.
241 First Avenue North
Minneapolis, MN 55401 U.S.A.

Website address: www.lernerbooks.com

Library of Congress Cataloging-in-Publication Data

Kerns, Ann, 1959–
    Did castles have bathrooms? : and other questions about
the Middle Ages / by Ann Kerns.
        p.   cm. — (Is that a fact?)
    Includes bibliographical references and index.
    ISBN 978–0–7613–4915–0 (lib. bdg. : alk. paper)
    1. Middle Ages—Juvenile literature. 2. Europe—
History—476-1492—Juvenile literature. 3. Europe—
Social life and customs—Juvenile literature. 4. Civilization,
Medieval—Juvenile literature. I. Title.
CB351.K39 2011
909.07—dc22   2009050429

Manufactured in the United States of America
1 – CG – 7/15/10